JBIOG
Coust 04-8-09
Petrie, Kristin

Jacques Cousteau

CHECKERBOARD BIOGRAPHY LIBRARY

EXPLORERS

Jacques
Cousteau

Kristin Petrie

ABDO
Publishing Company

visit us at
www.abdopub.com

Published by ABDO Publishing Company, 4940 Viking Drive, Edina, Minnesota 55435.
Copyright © 2004 by Abdo Consulting Group, Inc. International copyrights reserved in all
countries. No part of this book may be reproduced in any form without written permission from
the publisher.

Printed in the United States.

Cover Photos: Corbis
Interior Photos: AP/Wide World p. 9; Corbis pp. 5, 7, 8, 11, 13, 14, 15, 17, 20, 21, 23, 24, 25, 26,
    27, 29; Getty Images pp. 12, 16

Series Coordinator: Stephanie Hedlund
Editors: Kate A. Conley, Kristin Van Cleaf
Art Direction & Cover Design: Neil Klinepier
Interior Design & Maps: Dave Bullen

Library of Congress Cataloging-in-Publication Data

Petrie, Kristin, 1970-
    Jacques Cousteau / Kristin Petrie.
        p. cm. -- (Explorers.)
    Includes index.
    Summary: Examines the life and accomplishments of the French oceanographer, describing
his work studying and filming the undersea world.
    ISBN 1-59197-599-9
    1. Cousteau, Jacques Yves--Juvenile literature. 2. Oceanographers--France--Biography--
Juvenile literature. [1. Cousteau, Jacques Yves. 2. Oceanographers. 3. Scientists.] I. Title.

GC30.C68P48 2004
551.46'092--dc22
[B]   2003062923

Contents

Jacques Cousteau

A young French boy named Jacques Cousteau loved the water. At first, he just loved to swim and play. But soon, his enjoyment grew into something more. He became curious.

Jacques wanted to see what lay under the ocean's surface. But, the salt water stung his eyes. He also wanted to stay under water longer. But, he could only hold his breath for a short time.

Jacques was determined to overcome these obstacles. His **inquisitive** nature and talent for invention helped him do this. Jacques Cousteau was on his way to being the world's most well-known **oceanographer**, **environmentalist**, and filmmaker.

1451
Christopher Columbus born

1485
Hernán Cortés born

1450
John Cabot born

1460
Vasco da Gama born

1491
Jacques Cartier born

Jacques
Cousteau

1492
Columbus's first voyage west for Spain

1496
Cabot's first voyage for England

1493
Columbus's second voyage, attempted to colonize Hispaniola

Childhood

St.-André-de-Cubzac, France, was the hometown of Daniel and Elizabeth Cousteau. The couple's second son, Jacques-Yves Cousteau, was born there on June 11, 1910. A few weeks later, Elizabeth brought Jacques and his older brother to Paris.

In Paris, Daniel worked as a legal adviser for an American millionaire, Eugene Higgins. Daniel's work was filled with travel. He brought his family on all of his business trips. They traveled throughout Europe and to the United States.

Unfortunately, Jacques was often sick. Doctors told the Cousteaus to limit his activity. Higgins disagreed with the doctors. He thought exercise would improve Jacques's health. Higgins suggested that the Cousteaus let Jacques swim, and he even taught Jacques how.

1497
Cabot's second voyage, discovered the Grand Banks; da Gama was first to sail around Africa to India

1496 or 1497
Hernando de Soto born

1498
Cabot's third voyage, may have died; Columbus's third voyage

Jacques was in heaven. He'd always had a fascination with water. He wondered why some things floated. He wanted to know where bubbles came from and how fish breathed. Now, Jacques was able to be in the water as much as he liked.

The Cousteaus lived in Paris, France. The Eiffel Tower is one of Paris's landmarks.

1502
Columbus's fourth voyage; da Gama's second voyage

1506
Columbus died

1504
Cortés sailed to the West Indies

Expelled

When Jacques was ten, the Cousteaus moved to the United States. They lived there for two years. One summer, Jacques and his brother attended a camp in Vermont. There, Jacques learned the art of diving.

Cousteau's interest in machines helped him advance the art of diving.

For his first lesson, Jacques was told to dive to the bottom of the lake. He was to clean up the branches under the diving board. He loved this job and tried to stay under water for as long as possible.

As he grew older, Jacques's interests grew. He developed a passion for machines. His favorite was

1511
Cortés helped take over Cuba

1510
Francisco Vásquez de Coronado born

1514
De Soto went to the New World

the newly invented movie camera. Jacques saved his money and bought one when he was just 13 years old. He immediately took it apart to see how it worked, and then put it back together.

Around this time, Jacques began to lose interest in school. He was considered a poor student and was even **expelled** for bad behavior. Eventually, his parents sent him to a **strict** boarding school. Its **discipline** was just what Jacques needed. He did well and graduated at the age of 19.

Would You?

Would you enjoy diving like Cousteau? What is one thing you would like to learn about the ocean?

Navy Man

After graduation, Cousteau needed to choose a career. He knew he wanted to keep traveling, so he joined France's navy. Cousteau studied at a naval **academy** in Brest, France. Part of his training was spent aboard a ship that sailed around the world.

From 1933 to 1935, Cousteau sailed with the navy to the Far East. He was stationed at a base in Shanghai, China. From there, he was sent on **surveying** missions aboard a navy cruiser.

Cousteau decided flying would be his next challenge. So, he enrolled in the navy's **aviation** academy. However, a car accident in 1936 badly damaged his arms. After that, he could not become a pilot. Instead, Cousteau was assigned to a naval base in Toulon, France, where he taught courses.

1524
Da Gama's third voyage, died in Cochin, India

1519–1521
Cortés conquered the Aztec Empire and claimed Mexico for Spain

1532
De Soto helped attack the Inca Empire

Would You?

Would you like to travel around the world with the navy? What do you think Cousteau liked best about this job?

Cousteau was stationed in Shanghai, China, for two years.

A New Calling

Cousteau soon met a lieutenant named Philippe Tailliez. Tailliez advised Cousteau to swim in the Mediterranean Sea to strengthen his arms. Soon, they met up with a **civilian** named Frédéric Dumas. The three men shared a love of the ocean and a curiosity about the underwater world.

One day, Cousteau put on a pair of **aviation** goggles to look around under water. He was amazed by what he saw. Exploring beneath the water's surface became an interest for all three men. They began experimenting with diving and breathing devices.

At this time, divers used equipment such as heavy iron suits and hoses. The hoses

Cousteau with an iron diving suit

1534
Cartier's first voyage for France

1539–1542
De Soto explored La Florida

1533
De Soto helped take over Cuzco

1535
Cartier's second voyage

connected divers to their boats so they could receive oxygen while under water. Cousteau's mind reeled with the possibilities of "free" diving. He needed to invent a portable breathing machine.

For a while, however, Cousteau's mind wandered. He had met a young woman. Jacques Cousteau and Simone Melchior were married on July 12, 1937. The couple had two boys in the following years. Jean-Michel and Philippe both shared their parents' love of the sea and diving.

Jacques with his wife Simone

Spying

Cousteau and his friends continued their underwater experiments. Then in 1939, Adolf Hitler and his German army invaded Poland and **World War II** began.

Soon, Italy became **allied** with the German forces, and France joined the war against them. The Cousteaus remained unaffected by this change, but only for a short time.

In June 1940, Cousteau was sent to sea on the *Dupleix*. The ship was to sail up the coast and open fire on Genoa, Italy.

Adolf Hitler

After completing this assignment, the *Dupleix* safely returned to Toulon. Hitler's army, however, had seized Paris. The French surrendered to the Germans on June 22, 1940.

**The *Dupleix* was part of this French Mediterranean war fleet.
The fleet was based in Toulon, France, in the 1930s and 1940s.**

After the surrender, Cousteau was assigned to guard duty near Toulon. There was little military activity at the fort, and the Cousteaus again had a relatively normal life. They kept diving, and they fed themselves with fish and other seafood.

Secretly, however, Cousteau was still fighting the war. He had joined the French Resistance. This group was working against the German occupation in France. Cousteau's assignments involved underwater spying.

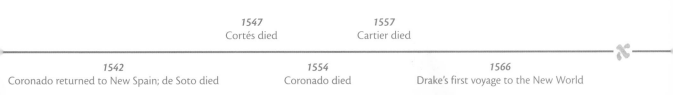

1547
Cortés died

1557
Cartier died

1542
Coronado returned to New Spain; de Soto died

1554
Coronado died

1566
Drake's first voyage to the New World

The Aqua-Lung

Because of his involvement with the French Resistance, Cousteau was more determined than ever. He needed to make deeper dives and stay under water longer.

In 1942, Cousteau returned to Paris and joined forces with Émile Gagnan. Gagnan was a brilliant engineer and an expert on gas equipment. He and Cousteau developed the Aqua-Lung.

Divers help Cousteau get ready to demonstrate the Aqua-Lung.

This device had two tanks of **compressed air**, which were worn on a diver's back. Hoses connected the tanks to a mouthpiece. A special **regulator** delivered the compressed air to the diver as he or she breathed.

1567
Drake's second voyage

1577
Drake began a worldwide voyage, was first Englishman to sail the Pacific Ocean

1570 and 1572
Drake terrorized the Spanish in the New World

After a few trials, Cousteau's dream was a reality. With the Aqua-Lung, he could dive deep into the water. He didn't have to hurry back to the surface for air. And, there were no long hoses to tangle him. So, he was free to roam and explore the underwater world.

Cousteau, Tailliez, and Dumas enjoyed this new device immensely. They made hundreds of dives. They tested the limits of the Aqua-Lung, as well as their bodies.

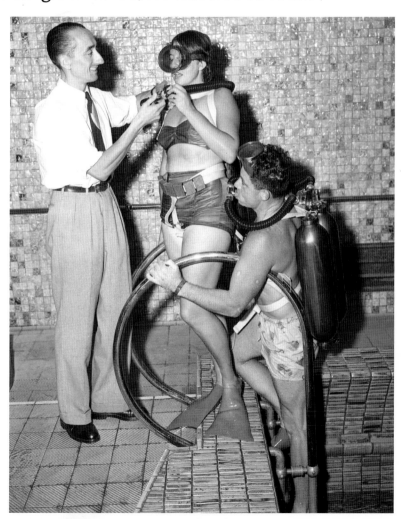

The Aqua-Lung could be used by anyone, not just professional divers.

Places Visited by Jacques Cousteau

ASIA

NORTH AMERICA

Shanghai

Singapore

Pacific Ocean

Great Barrier Reef

Indian Ocean

AUSTRALIA

Easter Island

Southern Ocean

ANTARCTICA

EUROPE

Brest
St.-André-de-Oubes
Paris
Genoa
Toulon

Mississippi River

St. Lawrence River

Atlantic Ocean

Mediterranean Sea

Nile River

Red Sea

AFRICA

Amazon River

SOUTH
AMERICA

Indian Ocean

Southern Ocean

ANTARCTICA

Brilliant Colors

During their experiments, the group took photos and made films of their dives. They improved underwater photography as they went.

Cousteau was the first person to bring light to the dark ocean floor. Before this, they had thought it was a world of dark shadows. They found it was really full of brilliant colors.

The pink starfish (*above*) and triggerfish (*opposite page*) show the many colors under water.

The public's first glimpse of this beautiful new world was through Cousteau's film *Eighteen Meters Down*. Later films included *Danger Under the Sea* and *Landscapes of Silence*. Eventually, he would make over 115 films about the ocean.

1588
Drake helped England win the Battle of Gravelines against Spain's Invincible Armada

1581
Drake knighted by Queen Elizabeth I

1596
Drake died

After the war, Cousteau demonstrated the Aqua-Lung to the navy. He soon received **permission** to begin diving experiments. The navy assigned the Underwater Research Group to Tailliez and Cousteau. The group soon got to work.

UNDERWATER RESEARCH GROUP'S ASSIGNMENTS

● ●

The Underwater Research Group was given a variety of assignments. One task was to defuse underwater bombs and live torpedoes left over from World War II.

The group also explored the insides of sunken ships. These dives showed that shipwrecks were places of great activity for sea creatures and plant life. As usual, the group recorded all of its work.

1728
James Cook born

1765
Boone journeyed to Florida

1768
Cook sailed for Tahiti

1734
Daniel Boone born

1767
Boone explored Kentucky

The Calypso

There was so much to uncover in the underwater world. Cousteau felt it was time to go farther into the waters. He left the navy and purchased the *Calypso*. It was a navy **minesweeping** ship that he converted into a high-tech research vessel.

On November 24, 1951, the *Calypso* set sail on its first expedition in the Red Sea. On board were Cousteau and his wife, Tailliez, and Dumas. Joining their close-knit group were several scientists.

During their years of exploring, the group filmed every amazing find. They wanted to share these hidden treasures with the world. They also knew funding for future expeditions would depend on the films they created.

In 1953, Cousteau wrote a book from his ship's logs. It was called *The Silent World*, and it was followed with a film of the same name in 1955. These accounts of the underwater world made Jacques Cousteau famous.

The film *The Silent World* won awards in France and the United States. The French government offered the group financial support. Soon, Cousteau also had support from the National Geographic Society in the United States and other sources.

The *Calypso*

1778
Cook became the first European to record Hawaiian Islands; Boone captured by Shawnee

1775
Boone cut the Wilderness Road from Virginia to Kentucky

1779
Cook died

Environmentalist

Cousteau's successful films provided him with the funds to continue inventing. In the 1950s, Cousteau and his crew developed a bathyscaphe, or diving saucer. By 1959, they had a successful version.

A diving saucer is loaded onto a truck.

The bathyscaphe was a two-person machine. It could stay under water for six hours and go 1,148 feet (350 m) below the surface. The diving saucer allowed Cousteau to explore even deeper in the ocean.

In the 1960s, space exploration was reaching new heights. Cousteau set out to prove that humans could live under water as well as in space. Between 1962 and 1965,

1813
John C. Frémont born

1842
Frémont's first independent surveying mission

1820
Boone died

"aquanauts" lived in several underwater "houses" for as long as a month!

Each new device helped develop a better understanding of marine life. Cousteau knew he needed to protect this fragile world. He became a passionate **environmentalist**.

Cousteau used television to alert the public to his cause. In 1968, the *Undersea World of Jacques Cousteau* began airing on ABC. The show lasted nine years. Then in 1974, Jacques Cousteau formed the Cousteau Society, which still works to protect marine life.

An aquanaut's underwater research center in the Red Sea

Would You?

Would you want to be an aquanaut? What do you think it would be like to live under water for a month?

Later Years

Soon, Cousteau's team developed an interest in the rivers that feed the oceans. So in 1978, they **surveyed** the Nile. In 1982 and 1983, Cousteau explored the Amazon River region, and later the Mississippi.

In 1985, Cousteau launched the *Alcyone*. It was newer and used less fuel than the *Calypso*. That same year, the crew set sail on a five-year, around-the-world tour with the *Alcyone*. They studied the relationship between people and the ocean environment.

Cousteau continued his life of exploration and diving. These years were not easy, however. In 1979, Cousteau had lost his son, Philippe. Then his wife of 53 years, Simone, died

Philippe Cousteau

1856
Frémont ran for president of the United States but lost

1845-1846
Frémont explored the Great Basin and the Pacific Coast, fought in the Mexican War

1890
Frémont died

The *Calypso* sailed up the St. Louis River after exploring the Mississippi River.

of cancer in 1990. The final loss occurred in 1996, when the *Calypso* sank in Singapore.

In 1991, Cousteau remarried. He and his new wife, Francine Triplet, had two children named Diane and Pierre-Yves. Also in 1991, Jacques began a petition called *A Bill of Rights for Future Generations*. It addresses the long-term problems of pollution.

The Legend

At the age of 87, Cousteau's amazing career as an **oceanographer** ended. He was hospitalized in Paris for a **respiratory** illness. Sadly, he was unable to recover. Jacques-Yves Cousteau died on June 25, 1997.

During his lifetime, Cousteau was honored in many ways. France awarded him their highest military award for his work in the French Resistance. President John F. Kennedy presented him with the National Geographic Society's Special Gold Medal.

The United Nations awarded Cousteau with their International Environmental Prize. However, his biggest accomplishment may have come one year after his death. Surely, Jacques Cousteau smiled when the United Nations declared 1998 the Year of the Ocean.

1997
Cousteau died

1974
Cousteau formed the Cousteau Society to protect marine life

Would You?

Would you give Jacques Cousteau an award? What would it be and why would you give it to him?

Many of Jacques Cousteau's awards resulted from his research with the Cousteau Society. He started the society in 1974. Today, it has more than 100,000 members working to protect and improve the environment.

Glossary

academy - a private school in which specific subjects are taught.

allies - people or countries that agree to help each other in times of need.

aviation - having to do with the operation and navigation of aircraft.

civilian - a person who is not a member of the military.

compressed air - a special mixture of breathing gases that are stored in a tank.

discipline - training that teaches order and obedience.

environmentalist - a person concerned with problems of the environment, especially the effects of uncontrolled pollution on the earth.

expel - to force out.

inquisitive - asking many questions.

minesweeper - a ship used to search a harbor, sea, or other area to remove, disarm, or harmlessly explode mines laid by an enemy.

oceanographer - an expert in the study of oceans, seas, and marine life.

permission - formal consent.

regulator - a device that controls the amount or timing of air given by a machine.

respiratory - having to do with the system of organs involved with breathing.

strict - severely conforming to a principle or a condition.

survey - to measure a piece of land to determine its shape, area, and boundaries.

World War II - from 1939 to 1945, fought in Europe, Asia, and Africa. The United States, France, Great Britain, the Soviet Union, and their allies were on one side. Germany, Italy, Japan, and their allies were on the other side. The war began when Germany invaded Poland. The United States entered the war in 1941 after Japan bombed Pearl Harbor, Hawaii.

Saying It

bathyscaphe - BA-thih-skaf
Émile Gagnan - AY-meel GAH-nyah
Jacques-Yves Cousteau - ZHAHK-EEV koo-STOH
Philippe Tailliez - FEE-leep TEYE-ehz
Shanghai - SHAHNG-HEYE
Toulon - too-LAWN

Web Sites

To learn more about Jacques Cousteau, visit ABDO Publishing Company on the World Wide Web at **www.abdopub.com**. Web sites about Jacques Cousteau are featured on our Book Links page. These links are routinely monitored and updated to provide the most current information available.

Index